Table of Contents

www.hewontknowitspaleo.com

For Daniel, David, Cara, and Micah

Creating traditions and memories with you is one of my favorite parts of motherhood.
You four make every holiday fun and full of love. I love you!

Photo Credit: Tara Holleman

Tips for a successful **AIP** Holiday

If you are not familiar with the Paleo Autoimmune Protocol (AIP), it is a version of the paleo diet that has shown great success in reducing inflammation and symptoms in autoimmune sufferers. Just because it carries many restrictions, however, does not mean it has to lack in flavor or comfort! This mini-cookbook provides a full menu for holidays that is completely compliant with the autoimmune protocol. Thank you to my loyal followers for all of your support – your success stories with AIP and my recipes inspire me to keep doing what I love to do: create recipes that are simple, delicious, and nourishing!

For you (the AIP diet follower):

1. Decide your must-haves. If the thought of a Thanksgiving without pumpkin pie makes you want to cry, make sure there is an AIP-compliant pie waiting for you at the end of your meal. I have come to accept that I may not be able to eat everything on the holiday spread, but I make sure I bring my personal must-haves so that I feel satisfied and not left out–even if that means only a few options for me.

2. Make sure every dish has its own serving utensils. This keeps people from using Aunt Sue's cornbread spatula in your AIP dressing, which could put you at risk for cross-contamination.

3. If you have a serving line, place your prepared dishes away from ones you know would cause you to react. This keeps the crumbs from the rolls from falling into your hard-earned AIP gravy.

4. Don't stress or feel sorry for yourself. You are healing your body, and that is something to get excited about! Enjoy what you *can* eat, and focus on the people around the table rather than the forbidden foods on top of it.

For them (the non-AIP diet followers):

1. "Let them eat cake." Or, in this case, let them bring food. It might make your insides turn and bring back unpleasant memories of poor eating and poorer health, but remember it's their holiday, too. Some restrictions may work for your family; for example, you or your child may have celiac disease and you always keep your home gluten-free. Your family may be totally on board with that. But unless your family wins the "Most Awesome Family Ever" award by cooking 100 percent AIP foods, requiring everyone to cook paleo or AIP foods will likely leave people frustrated.

2. If it's going to cause strife, keep your diet on the down-low. I know AIP is a huge deal to us autoimmune sufferers but, let's be honest, unless someone has a chronic illness, they are not likely to understand why you eat the way you do. I try to keep my personal intolerances and food issues to myself and not make it a topic of conversation. Some people will think it's awesome that you eat so well, and some people will think it's crazy. All in all, I find it best to avoid needless food controversies during holiday gatherings. (P.S. This is one of the reasons I titled my blog and cookbook, "He Won't Know It's Paleo." I knew my Southern husband would not want to eat paleo or AIP, so I just started feeding him that way without telling him. I finally told him after six months. If you want to cook your AIP foods and not tell anyone, I promise I'll keep your secret, too! Oh, and that husband of mine? He eats mostly paleo now–by choice. ☺)

3. Have fun! Have some board games or a fun outdoor game of football ready to play after dinner. It will keep you from eyeing restricted foods, and you'll all have a great time playing together.

Simple Turkey & Gravy

Prep Time: 30 minutes
Cook Time: 2-3 hours

Brining Time: 8 hours
Yield: 10-12 servings

There are endless ways to cook a turkey, but I find I prefer it best to let the turkey flavor shine through by seasoning it simply and roasting it to perfection. Since using a pastured bird may mean some loss of tenderness, I use a dry brine to help soften the fibers and yield a juicy and tender bird.

Ingredients:

For the Turkey:
1 (10- to 12-pound) turkey, thawed
1/3 cup sea salt
1/2 teaspoon dried, rubbed sage
avocado oil

For the Gravy:
turkey drippings, plus enough turkey broth to make 3-5 cups of total liquid (see broth directions below)
2 tablespoons arrowroot flour
pinch dried rubbed sage, optional
sea salt to taste

Directions:

For the turkey:
1. The day before (at least 8 hours before) cooking, remove the turkey neck and organs. Set aside for broth. (See directions below.) Rinse the thawed turkey with cold water and pat dry.
2. Mix together the salt and sage. Rub the mixture into entire turkey inside and out. Truss the bird, if desired. (Trussing tutorials can be easily found online.) Place the uncovered turkey into the refrigerator overnight or for at least 8 hours.
3. When ready to cook, preheat the oven to 325°F.
4. Place the turkey, breast up, on a rack in a roasting pan. Rub or brush the skin of the turkey with avocado oil. Roast it in the oven for 13-15 minutes per pound, or until a thermometer reaches 165°F. Remove the turkey from the oven, set it on a serving platter, and let it rest before carving while you make the gravy.

For the turkey broth:
1. While the turkey is brining or roasting, place 1 tablespoon of avocado oil into a medium saucepan. Cook the turkey neck and organs for 5-7 minutes over low to medium heat. Turn occasionally to brown all sides. When they are finished cooking, add 6 cups of water plus 1 1/2 teaspoons sea salt. Bring to a boil, then simmer on low for 2-4 hours, or while the turkey roasts. Tip: You can also make this overnight in a crockpot for a richer flavor. Prepare the same way as described, but after you bring the pot to a boil, place all of the saucepan ingredients into a crockpot, and cook on low for 8 hours.

For the gravy:
1. Skim the separated grease from the top of the drippings in the roasting pan. Set the roasting pan over double burners on the stovetop. Add enough broth to make about 3 to 5 cups of total liquid. Whisk in the arrowroot flour and sage until completely dissolved.
2. Turn the burners on medium. Whisk while the liquid is heating and scrape up the brown bits from the bottom of the pan. Bring the mixture to a simmer, while whisking, until the gravy thickens. Remove from heat, and season with sea salt to taste. Pour into a gravy boat to serve.

Prime Rib Au Jus

Prep Time: 15 minutes   Resting Time: 2-3 hours   Cook Time: 1 hour
Yield: 8-10 servings

This roast is simple to put together, but yields one of the best entrées you'll ever cook up! I love to give prime rib the spotlight on Christmas after Thanksgiving is over and turkey was already enjoyed. Since prime rib roasts are a more expensive cut of meat, I highly recommend investing in a reputable internal meat thermometer to make sure you get it perfect.

Ingredients:

For the Roast:
1 (5 pound) prime rib roast
1 tablespoon sea salt
1 1/2 teaspoons dried, crushed rosemary
3 tablespoons avocado oil

For the Au Jus:
3 cups beef stock or bone broth
2 tablespoons red wine (optional)
brown bits from the bottom of the roasting pan

Directions:

For the Roast:

1. Two to three hours before cooking, take the roast out of the refrigerator. Unwrap it, place it on a plate, and let it rest until it reaches room temperature.
2. Once the roast is at room temperature, preheat the oven to 500°F. Place the roast fatty-side up (or rib-side down) in a roasting pan. No rack is needed since the ribs will serve as a rack.
3. In a small bowl, mix together the salt and rosemary. Rub the avocado oil over the entire prime rib, especially over the cut ends. Follow with the salt and rosemary mixture.
4. Bake the roast for 15 minutes at 500°F or until a crust forms on the top of the meat, then reduce the temperature to 325°F. Continue to roast at 325°F for 40-50 minutes, until it reaches an internal temperature of 135 F.
5. Remove the roast from the oven, and transfer it to a serving platter. Let it rest for 15 minutes before carving to allow the juices to evenly distribute. (Don't skip the resting part! Carving too soon after roasting will cause a significant loss of juice.)

For the Au Jus:

1. While the roast is resting on the platter, place the roasting pan on the stovetop with double burners turned on high heat. Add the stock or broth and red wine. Use a whisk to scrape up the brown bits from the bottom of the pan as it boils. Boil 6-8 minutes, until slightly reduced. Transfer the au jus to a gravy boat for serving.

Pastured Honey Ham

Prep Time: 30 minutes   Brining Time: 1-3 days   Cook Time: 8 hours
Yield: 12-14 servings

Slow-cooked to tender perfection, this Honey Ham is sure to leave all of your guests going back for seconds. To achieve a juicy, tender ham, this recipe brines the ham and slow-cooks it to ensure a tender, to-die-for result. To use a precooked ham, see the note at the end.

Ingredients:

For the Brine:

1 cup pear juice
1 cup pineapple juice
1 yellow onion, quartered
3 cloves garlic, halved
1 tablespoon whole cloves
1 bunch fresh rosemary
1/2 cup sea salt
3 tablespoons smoked sea salt
1 gallon water

For the Ham:

1 (6 to 8-pound) uncooked pastured ham shank OR 1 precooked (AIP-ingredient-friendly) cooked ham (if using precooked, read footnote for directions)
1 tablespoon whole cloves (optional)

For the Glaze:

1/2 cup honey
1/4 cup pineapple juice
1/4 cup pear juice
1/2 teaspoon onion powder
1/2 teaspoon garlic powder
1/4 teaspoon ground cloves

Directions:

For brining the ham:

1. 24 to 72 hours before cooking the ham, score the skin and fat diagonally in 1-inch intervals. Be careful not to pierce the meat beneath. Repeat in the opposite direction, making diamond shapes in the skin. Insert cloves in the corners, as shown.
2. Place the ham in a bowl or basin large enough to hold the entire ham and a gallon of water.
3. Pour all of the brine ingredients, except for the water, over the ham. Fill the bowl with the gallon of water, or just enough water to cover the entire ham, and cover it with plastic wrap. Place the ham in the refrigerator for 1-3 days.

For baking the ham:

1. Preheat the oven to 225°F.
2. Place the ham, with the fat and skin facing up, in a roasting pan.
3. Roast the ham in the oven for 8 hours, or about an hour per pound. The ham is done when it reaches an internal temperature of 145-150°F and the meat begins to loosen around the bone.

For the glaze:

1. Whisk together the honey, juices, garlic powder, onion powder and cloves in a saucepan. Bring to a boil, uncovered, over medium heat. Reduce heat to medium-low and simmer 7-8 minutes, or until liquid is thickened and reduced by half. Remove from the heat, cover, and refrigerate until the ham is finished cooking.
2. When the ham is finished, remove it from the oven. Brush the glaze over the top, and increase the heat to 400°F. Return ham to the oven and bake for 8-10 minutes, or until the glaze has browned and caramelized. Remove the ham from the oven, and let it rest 10 minutes before carving.

Want to use a precooked ham? First, check the ingredients to make sure they are AIP-compliant. These hams are often available before major holidays at health-food stores like Whole Foods. For a precooked ham, skip the brining and baking directions. Use the brine ingredients as a basting liquid (except for the water and salts; omit those). Shake the brine ingredients together in a jar and refrigerate for 12-48 hours. Bake the ham according to the directions on the package but, during baking, baste the ham with the refrigerated liquid every 20-30 minutes. Proceed to glaze directions for finishing.

Caesar Salad

Prep Time: 10 minutes
Yield: 8 servings

Ingredients:

For the dressing:
2/3 cup avocado oil
1 tablespoon olive oil
2 tablespoons lemon juice
1 teaspoon fish sauce
2 medium garlic cloves, peeled
1/4 teaspoon sea salt

For the salad:
8 cups rinsed and chopped romaine hearts
chopped artichoke hearts, canned (optional)
hearts of palm, canned (optional)
black olives (optional)

Directions:

1. In a blender, combine the dressing ingredients. Blend on high until smooth and creamy. Refrigerate in a lidded jar and shake to combine before serving. If the oils have solidified in the refrigerator, remove the dressing from the refrigerator 15 minutes before serving.
2. Toss the dressing with the salad ingredients just before serving.

Tip: Top your salad with leftover turkey or prime rib for a protein-rich meal after the holiday is over!

Grandma Joyce's Dressing

Prep Time: 30 minutes   Cook Time: 45 minutes
Yield: 12-14 servings

This AIP version of my grandmother's much-adored dressing recipe is one of my most proud-of recipe conversions. My grandmother used the married flavors of bacon and sage to create a flavorful, savory side that pairs perfectly with turkey and gravy.

Ingredients:

8 ounces bacon
1/2 cup bacon grease (rendered from the cooked bacon, plus any additional grease needed to total 1/2 cup of grease)
2 1/2 pounds white-fleshed sweet potatoes, peeled and chopped into 1/2-inch pieces (Orange sweet potatoes are not starchy enough for this recipe.)
3/4 cup chicken or turkey stock, or bone broth
1 1/2 teaspoons salt
1 1/2 teaspoons dried rubbed sage
1 teaspoon baking soda
1 large yellow onion, chopped
2 cups celery, chopped
2 Gelatin Egg Substitutes, prepared when directed (See recipe page 36.)
1 tablespoon apple cider vinegar

Directions:

1. Preheat the oven to 350°F. Grease a 9- by 13-inch baking dish with bacon grease or avocado oil.
2. In a large skillet over medium heat, cook bacon until the fat is rendered, about 7-8 minutes. Keep 1/2 cup of the grease in the pan, and set the bacon aside to cool. If the bacon did not render 1/2 cup of grease, add additional bacon grease, tallow, palm shortening or other heat-stable oil to make 1/2 cup of total fat. I do not recommend coconut oil here since it might add a coconut flavor.
3. In a food processor, process the chopped sweet potatoes until a thick paste forms with no clumps. This may need to be done in two batches, depending on the size of the processor. Add the chicken stock, salt, sage, and baking soda to the processed sweet potato. Process again until thoroughly combined. (If the processor is not large enough and two batches are needed, combine these ingredients together in a large mixing bowl.) Set aside.
4. Add the onion and celery to the bacon grease skillet. Sauté on medium heat until the vegetables are transparent, about 10 minutes. Stir occasionally and scrape up the brown bits.
5. Prepare the gelatin egg substitutes. Add them, and the apple cider vinegar, to the food processor or mixing bowl. Process or stir until the gelatin egg substitutes are thoroughly mixed in.
6. Add the sautéed celery, onions, and all of the bacon grease into the sweet potato mixture. Crumble in the bacon. Stir until uniformly combined.
7. Spread the mixture into the prepared baking dish. Bake for 45-50 minutes, until the edges are golden brown and a toothpick inserted into the center comes out clean. Do not over bake. Serve hot.

Make-ahead tip: Prepare and bake a day in advance. Store loosely covered in the refrigerator. To serve warm, reheat at 350°F for 20 minutes, until hot throughout. I actually prefer this dish the second day.

Roasted and Mashed Fauxtatoes

Prep Time: 15 minutes   Cook Time: 45 minutes

Yield: 6 servings

Mashed potatoes and holidays just go together. But when you have a nightshade intolerance, this can really put a damper on the fluff under the gravy. This recipe creates a good imposter that adds in great nutrients, too!

Ingredients:

- 2 heads cauliflower, core removed and cut into florets
- 3 cloves garlic, peeled and halved
- 1 tablespoon avocado oil, plus 2 tablespoons avocado oil for blending
- 1 small white-fleshed sweet potato or 1 parsnip, peeled and coarsely chopped
- 1 teaspoon of truffle salt or sea salt

Directions:

1. Preheat the oven to 350°F.
2. Toss 1/4 of the cauliflower and all of the garlic with a tablespoon of avocado oil. Spread them in a single layer on a baking sheet, and bake until caramelized, about 25 minutes.
3. Meanwhile, bring a large pot of water to a boil. Add the remaining cauliflower and sweet potato or parsnip to the boiling water. Boil for 20 minutes or until the vegetables are tender.
4. Drain the vegetables, shake off as much liquid as possible, and discard the water. Return the cooked vegetables to the pot.
5. Add the roasted cauliflower and garlic, remaining oil, and salt. Blend with an immersion blender or transfer to a blender and blend until smooth and creamy.

Mama E's Squash Casserole

Prep Time: 10 minutes   Cook Time: 45 minutes
Yield: 10-12 servings

Ever since I married my husband, I looked forward to his grandmother's squash casserole on holidays. Once I went paleo and AIP, however, I could no longer enjoy the crackers, milk, and cheese that went into it. This version brings a delicious and nutrient-packed spin on my old favorite, and I must say I enjoy it just as much.

Ingredients:

avocado oil for greasing the pan
4 zucchini squash, quartered lengthwise and sliced
4 yellow squash, quartered lengthwise and sliced
1 yellow onion, chopped
1 small carrot, peeled and quartered lengthwise (creating long thin strips)
3/4 cup coconut milk
1 tablespoon arrowroot flour
1 teaspoon sea salt
1 cup plantain chips, crushed

Directions:

1. Preheat the oven to 350°F and grease a 9- by 13-inch dish with avocado oil.
2. Bring a large pot of water to a boil. Add the squash, onion, and carrot. Boil for 10-12 minutes, until the squash and onion are translucent and the carrot is tender. Drain the vegetables and discard the water.
3. Using a fork, separate the carrot pieces from the remaining vegetables. Add the carrots, coconut milk, arrowroot flour, and sea salt to a blender. Blend on high until the mixture is a yellow liquid. Set aside.
4. Mash the zucchini and onion mixture with a potato masher, and drain it again to remove any excess water. Return the squash mixture to the pot or a large mixing bowl, and gently stir in the blended carrot liquid. Spread the mixture into the prepared baking dish.
5. Sprinkle the crushed plantain chips evenly over the top. Bake for 30 minutes, until the yellow liquid is bubbly and thickened.

Make-ahead Tip: Prepare the entire casserole omitting the plantain chips. Cover tightly and refrigerate up to a day in advance. Just before baking, add the crushed plantain chips.

Carrot Casserole

Prep Time: 10 minutes   Cook Time: 35-40 minutes
Yield: 10-12 servings

My grandmother always made a cheesy, cracker-crumb-topped carrot casserole that was to die for. This version is still delicious and makes me feel like I'm enjoying her casserole all over again.

Ingredients:

2 pounds carrots, peeled and chopped
2 tablespoons avocado oil for sautéing the onion, plus 1/4 cup for the sauce
1 medium yellow onion, diced
3/4 cup coconut milk
1 tablespoon arrowroot flour
1 teaspoon sea salt, plus more for sprinkling
1 cup plantain chips, crushed

Directions:

1. Preheat the oven to 350°F. Grease a 9- by 13-inch baking dish with avocado oil.
2. Bring a large pot of water to a boil. Add the carrots and boil until they are just tender enough to push a fork through, about 10-15 minutes. When finished cooking, strain and discard the water. Reserve 1/4 cup of the cooked carrots and set aside. Spread the remaining carrots in the bottom of the prepared baking dish.
3. While the carrots are boiling, heat two tablespoons of the oil over medium heat in a large frying pan. Add the diced onion. Sauté for 10-15 minutes until the onions are translucent and beginning to brown. Gently combine the sautéed onions and the cooked carrots in the baking dish.
4. In a blender, blend the reserved 1/4 cup of cooked carrots, 1/4 cup of avocado oil, coconut milk, arrowroot flour, and sea salt until smooth and creamy. Pour the mixture evenly over the carrots and onions in the baking dish.
5. Sprinkle the top of the casserole with the crushed plantain chips. Bake for 25 minutes, until the liquid is thickened and bubbly.

Make-ahead Tip: Prepare the entire casserole, omitting the plantain chips. Cover tightly and refrigerate up to a day in advance. Just before baking, add the crushed plantain chips.

Egg-Free Sweet Potato Soufflé

Prep Time: 10 minutes   Cook Time: 20 minutes
Yield: 6 servings

Another one of Mama E's famous recipes, this side brings a dessert-like spin on sweet potatoes. Even those who don't love sweet potatoes will likely enjoy this dish.

Ingredients

3 pounds orange-flesh sweet potatoes or kabocha squash, peeled and coarsely chopped
1/2 cup avocado oil, plus extra for greasing
1/2 cup coconut milk
3 tablespoons evaporated cane juice
1 teaspoon vanilla extract
1/2 teaspoon cinnamon
1/4 teaspoon ground cloves

Directions

1. Preheat the oven to 350°F. Grease an 8- by 8-inch casserole dish with avocado oil.
2. Fill a large pot halfway full with water and bring it to a boil. Add the sweet potatoes or squash and boil until tender, about 15-20 minutes. Drain, discard the water, and add the cooked sweet potatoes or squash to a large mixing bowl.
3. Add the remaining ingredients and mix on medium speed until smooth and creamy.
4. Spread the mixture into an 8- by 8-inch prepared casserole. If needed, reheat at 350°F for 5-10 minutes.

Make-ahead Tip: Prepare the dish entirely. Cover tightly and refrigerate for up to a day. Bake at 350°F for 20-30 minutes until hot throughout.

Pumpkin Pancakes and Waffles

Prep Time: 10 minutes   Cook Time: 8 minutes
Yield: 4 servings

Waffles and pancakes are a perfect treat during the holiday break. My kids love this recipe and I love being able to enjoy it with them!

Ingredients:

1/3 cup coconut flour
1/2 cup arrowroot flour
1/2 teaspoon sea salt
3/4 teaspoon baking soda
3/4 teaspoon cream of tartar
1 teaspoon ground cinnamon
1/4 teaspoon ground ginger
1/8 teaspoon ground cloves
2/3 cup coconut milk
1/4 cup coconut butter
1/4 cup pumpkin puree
2 tablespoons coconut oil, plus more for greasing
2 tablespoons maple syrup
1/2 teaspoon vanilla extract
1 1/2 teaspoons apple cider vinegar
1 Gelatin Egg Substitute, prepared when directed (See recipe page 36.)

Directions:

1. For pancakes, place a large frying pan over low heat and grease with coconut oil. For waffles, lightly grease and heat a waffle iron on low heat.
2. In a small mixing bowl, whisk together the coconut flour, arrowroot flour, sea salt, baking soda, cream of tartar, cinnamon, ginger, and cloves.
3. In a medium mixing bowl, whisk together the coconut milk, coconut butter, pumpkin, coconut oil, maple syrup, vanilla, and apple cider vinegar.
4. Add the dry ingredients to the wet ingredients and whisk until combined.
5. Prepare the gelatin egg substitute. Add it to the mixing bowl and whisk all ingredients together.

For pancakes:

Drop the batter by 1/4 cup onto the heated and greased pan, creating round, thin pancakes. Cook about 4 minutes, until the bubbles stop rising to the top and a spatula can easily slide under without breaking apart the pancake. Flip and cook another 3-4 minutes, until the pancakes are cooked throughout. Note: As the batter sits in the mixing bowl for subsequent batches, the gelatin egg substitute may begin to solidify. If this happens, gently press the batter with a rubber spatula to form thin, round pancakes.

For waffles:

When the waffle iron is preheated, drop 1/4 cup of batter into each greased section. Close the waffle iron and cook until the steam slows and the waffle iron can be opened easily without breaking the waffle apart. Carefully remove the waffles with a fork. Tip: I like to make "mini-waffle bites" by dropping random spoonfuls of batter in the waffle maker. These are easy to remove and do not break as easily.

Spiced Bread Pudding with Rum Cajeta Glaze

Prep Time: 10 minutes   Cook Time: 40 minutes   Yield: 12-16 servings

If there is a word to describe this dessert, it is *heavenly*. The flavors in this bread pudding have a "wow" factor, which few desserts possess, especially ones in a restricted diet! You can proudly bring this dessert to any gathering and the guests will be begging for the recipe.

Ingredients:

For the bread pudding:

2 1/2 pounds white-fleshed sweet potatoes, peeled and chopped into 1/2-inch pieces (Orange sweet potatoes are not starchy enough for this recipe.)

3 tablespoons coconut sugar

1/3 cup evaporated cane juice

3/4 cup full-fat coconut milk

1 teaspoon baking soda

1 teaspoon sea salt

1 teaspoon vanilla extract

1/2 cup palm shortening

3/4 teaspoon ground cloves

2 Gelatin Egg Substitutes, prepared when directed (See recipe page 36.)

1 tablespoon apple cider vinegar

For the Rum Cajeta Glaze:

1/2 cup honey

1 1/3 cups coconut milk

1/4 cup rum

1/2 teaspoon sea salt

Directions:

For the bread pudding:

1. Preheat the oven to 350°F. Grease a 9- by 13-inch baking dish.
2. In a food processor, pulse the sweet potatoes until a paste forms. This may need to be done in two batches, depending on the size of the processor. Add the remaining ingredients, with the exception of the gelatin egg substitutes and apple cider vinegar, to the processed sweet potato. Process again until thoroughly combined. (If the processor is not large enough and two batches are needed, combine the mixture together in a large mixing bowl.) Set aside.
3. Prepare the gelatin egg substitutes. Add them and the apple cider vinegar to the food processor and pulse or stir until thoroughly combined.
4. Pour the mixture into the prepared baking dish and bake for 40-45 minutes, or until the edges are golden-brown and a toothpick inserted into the center comes out clean.
5. Serve warm with Rum Cajeta Glaze (directions follow) drizzled over the top.

For the Rum Cajeta Glaze:

1. In a small saucepan, over medium-high heat, whisk together the honey, coconut milk, rum, and salt.
2. While whisking, bring the mixture to a full boil, uncovered. Reduce the heat to medium-low and simmer for 20 minutes. Stir occasionally, scraping the sides and bottom to avoid burning. (Makes 1/2 cup. Store refrigerated for up to one week. Gently warm and stir before use.)

Baklava Bites

Prep Time: 10 minutes   Cook Time: 15 minutes
Yield: 18 servings (36 bites)

These are a fun appetizer-like dessert that everyone will love. In fact, even my date-hating husband kept coming back and sneaking more bites last time I made them.

Ingredients

6 coconut wraps (pre-packaged and available on Amazon)
ground cinnamon
36 dates, pitted and minced
1 cup coconut oil
honey, optional

Directions

1. Cut each wrap into six long, equal strips about 1-inch wide.
2. Lightly dust the top side of the strips with cinnamon. Place 1/2 tablespoon of minced dates (about one date) onto one end of each strip. Tightly roll the dates into each. Pack the chopped dates back in as needed.
3. Heat the coconut oil in a small saucepan over medium heat, reducing the heat to low when the oil is melted and hot.
4. Brown the rolls, six at a time, in the heated coconut oil. Make sure the tail of the roll is facing down so that it does not unroll. If it begins to unroll, use a fork or small spatula to hold it together during cooking. Once the bottoms are golden brown, rotate the roll until the entire piece is golden brown. Remove rolls with tongs and cool on a wire rack, cut-side-down. Repeat with remaining rolls.
5. If desired, lightly drizzle with honey before serving.

Tip: If you tolerate nuts, you can replace 1/2 of the dates with 2/3 cups of finely chopped pecans. (Note: Nuts are a Stage 2 AIP reintroduction.)

Pumpkin Pie

Prep Time: 20 minutes   Cook Time: 17 minutes   Chill Time: 4 hours
Yield: 8 servings

For me, it isn't a holiday unless pumpkin pie is served. This version is completely AIP, but nobody will guess among the flavorful spices and great texture!

Ingredients:

For the pastry crust:

2/3 cup coconut flour
1/4 teaspoon sea salt
1/4 teaspoon baking soda
2/3 cup palm shortening
1 1/2 teaspoons maple syrup (optional)
2 Gelatin Egg Substitutes, prepared when directed (See recipe page 36.)

For the filling:

1 (13.5-ounce) can coconut milk
2 teaspoons gelatin
1 (15-ounce) can pumpkin puree
2/3 cup honey
3/4 teaspoon sea salt
1 1/2 teaspoons ground cinnamon
3/4 teaspoon ground ginger
1/4 teaspoon ground cloves
1/4 teaspoon ground mace

Directions:

For the pastry crust:

1. Preheat the oven to 350°F.
2. In a medium mixing bowl, whisk the coconut flour, salt, and baking soda. Add the palm shortening and optional maple syrup, and stir with a rubber spatula to combine.
3. Prepare the gelatin egg substitutes and add them to the crust mixture. Stir until completely incorporated. Press the dough into a 9-inch pie plate and flute the edges if desired. Bake for 15 to 17 minutes, until the edges are golden brown and the center is firm to the touch. Cool completely on a wire rack.

For the filling:

1. Whisk the gelatin and coconut milk in a small saucepan over medium-high heat, whisking frequently, until the mixture begins to boil and the gelatin is completely dissolved. Remove the saucepan from the heat and add in the remaining ingredients. Whisk until completely smooth and creamy.
2. Pour the mixture into the cooled crust. Refrigerate for 4 hours, until set and firm to the touch.

Make-ahead Tip: Make a day in advance. Store covered in the refrigerator.

The Healthy Mint Shake

Reminiscent of the sugar-laden Shamrock treat, this shake is the perfect breakfast or dessert, and no one (not even my 8-year-old) will guess there is a boatload of green spinach leaves inside! This is a favorite of my kids and I feel so good handing it to them, knowing it is healthy and full of nutrients!

Prep Time: 5 minutes   Yield: 1-2 shakes

Ingredients:

- 2/3 cup coconut milk
- 1/4 large avocado
- 2 handfuls spinach
- 1/4 teaspoon vanilla extract (alcohol-free)
- 1/4 teaspoon peppermint extract (alcohol-free) or 1-2 drops peppermint essential oil
- 2 tablespoons honey
- 1 cup crushed ice
- 2 tablespoons collagen, for added protein (optional)

Directions:

Place all the ingredients into a blender and blend on high until smooth and creamy.

Tip: If you tolerate chocolate, adding soy-free miniature chocolate chips will turn this smoothie into a healthy after-dinner dessert! (Note: Chocolate is a Stage 2 AIP reintroduction.)

Spiced Cranberry Sauce

Prep Time: 5 minutes   Cook Time: 15 minutes   Chill Time: 4 hours
Yield: 10 servings

I have converted many family and friends to this recipe over the years. The flavors are deep and complex, and it wonderfully compliments a holiday meal. To me it's the perfect cranberry sauce to share with all guests–paleo and non-paleo alike.

Ingredients:

3/4 cup honey
1/3 cup freshly-squeezed orange juice
1/3 cup water
1/4 teaspoon ground cloves
1/8 teaspoon sea salt
12 ounces fresh cranberries

Directions:

1. In a medium saucepan, combine honey, orange juice, water, cloves and sea salt. Bring mixture to a boil over high heat.
2. Add the cranberries, return to a boil, and reduce to medium-low heat. Boil gently for 10 minutes, uncovered. Transfer to a serving bowl and refrigerate for 4 hours, until completely cool and softly gelled.

Gingerbread Cookies

Prep Time: 20 minutes   Cook Time: 17-21 minutes   Yield: 18 cookies

Although this recipe is also in my main cookbook, I couldn't resist throwing it into this mini-cookbook because it is so much fun to make! Nothing says, "Christmas is coming!" quite like building a gingerbread house or decorating gingerbread cookies. My kids think making (and eating) these is a highlight of the holidays.

Ingredients:

For the Gingerbread:

1 cup coconut flour
1 1/2 teaspoons ground ginger
1 teaspoon cinnamon
1/2 teaspoon sea salt
1/2 teaspoon baking soda
1/2 cup palm shortening or coconut oil, softened
1/2 cup honey
1/4 cup blackstrap molasses
1 1/2 teaspoons vanilla
2 Gelatin Egg Substitutes, prepared when directed (See recipe page 36.)

For the frosting:

1 cup palm shortening
3/4 cup honey

For the décor:

dried cranberries, blueberries, and apricots
dried bananas
unsweetened, shredded coconut

Directions:

For the Gingerbread:

1. In a small bowl, whisk together the flour, ginger, cinnamon, salt, and baking soda.
2. In a large bowl or stand mixer, mix the shortening, honey, molasses, and vanilla on medium speed to combine.
3. Prepare the gelatin egg substitutes and add them to the wet mixture. Mix on medium speed just until the gelatin egg substitutes are incorporated.
4. Add the dry ingredients to the wet ingredients and mix on medium-high speed until thoroughly combined and creamy. Scrape the dough from the mixing bowl onto a large piece of parchment paper. Cover with a second large piece of parchment paper and roll to 1/4-inch thickness. (The two layers of parchment paper will prevent the dough from sticking to the surface or rolling pin.)

   For gingersnaps: Score into desired size with a pizza cutter.

   For cut-out cookies: Use cookie cutters to cut out shapes.

   For gingerbread house: Use the pattern on page 36.

5. Bake for 17 to 21 minutes, until cookies reach desired firmness. Cool completely on a wire rack before frosting or building.

   For the frosting:

   Beat the shortening and honey together on high until whipped and fluffy.

Gelatin Egg Substitute

Prep Time: 5 minutes
Yield: Substitute for 1 egg

While eggs are a nutritious part of a standard diet as well as a paleo diet, they are not part of the elimination stage of the Autoimmune Protocol because they can stimulate an immune response. This substitute does not create rise in baked goods like a real egg does, but it binds beautifully.

Ingredients:

1 tablespoon grass-fed gelatin
1 tablespoon lukewarm water
2 tablespoons boiling or very hot water

Directions:

1. Whisk the gelatin into lukewarm water. The mixture will create a rubbery gel.
2. Add the boiling water and whisk vigorously until completely dissolved and frothy. Use immediately. If it sits too long, it will solidify and be unusable.

Tip: If you tolerate eggs well (eggs are a Stage 2 AIP reintroduction), feel free to substitute one egg for each "gelatin egg substitute" called for throughout this book, with the exception of unbaked goods which require the use of gelatin to solidify (i.e. the pumpkin pie).

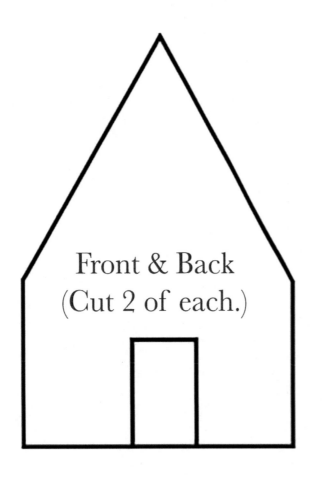

Front & Back
(Cut 2 of each.)

Roof
(Cut 2 of each.)

Sides
(Cut 2 of each.)

Hungry for more?

The following holiday recipes are from my full cookbook, *He Won't Know It's Paleo: 100+ Autoimmune Protocol Recipes to Create with Love and Share with Pride* available on Amazon.

About Bre'anna Emmitt

Bre'anna Emmitt is the author of the best-selling cookbook, *He Won't Know It's Paleo*. She uses her culinary successes to help others put the joy back in eating while following the Paleo Autoimmune Protocol (AIP). Since following the AIP lifestyle, Bre'anna has noticed drastic improvements in her two autoimmune diseases and finds great satisfaction in helping others work toward the same goal. When she's not in the kitchen, Bre'anna enjoys spending time with her husband, Chris, and their four children.

www.hewontknowitspaleo.com

Made in the USA
San Bernardino, CA
30 October 2016